Cocktails FOR DUMMIES®

MINI EDITION

by Ray Foley

Wiley Publishing, Inc.

Cocktails For Dummies,® Mini Edition

Published by
Wiley Publishing, Inc.
111 River St.
Hoboken, NJ 07030-5774
www.wiley.com

Published by Wiley Publishing, Inc., Indianapolis, Indiana

Published simultaneously in Canada

For general information on our other products and services, please contact our Customer Care Department within the U.S. at 877-762-2974, outside the U.S. at 317-572-3993, or fax 317-572-4002.

For technical support, please visit www.wiley.com/techsupport.

Wiley also publishes its books in a variety of electronic formats and by print-on-demand. Some content that appears in standard print versions of this book may not be available in other formats. For more information about Wiley products, visit us at www.wiley.com.

ISBN: 978-1-118-06165-7

Manufactured in the United States of America

10 9 8 7 6 5 4 3 2 1

Table of Contents

Introduction

When you hear the words "Set 'em up, Joe," you better have at least a basic knowledge of over 200 of the most called-for cocktails in your head. I say cocktails because a *cocktail* is, according to Webster, "any of various alcoholic drinks made of a distilled liquor mixed with a wine, fruit juice, etc., and usually iced."

In this book, I show you how to prepare and serve cocktails. You'll find all the recipes you need to mix cocktails for your guests. I show you the correct equipment to use and help you set up for parties.

You don't need any special knowledge of liquor or mixology to understand this book. Having an interest in creating crowd-pleasing cocktails is definitely a plus, and having the patience to get recipes just right doesn't hurt either. Good bartenders are always trying new things in the interest of serving the tastiest beverages.

A bartender cannot be made overnight, though, and a head full of recipes and facts will get you only so far. You need experience, and you must respect and like people. If you aren't a people person, all the great information in this book won't make you a bartender.

As a bartender for over 20 years, I always enjoyed the atmosphere and people in bars and restaurants. They are there to relax and have fun. My job was to serve and be a part of the entertainment, to make the guests feel at home and relaxed, never to be overbearing or intruding. So a good attitude and a lot of experience are key. From here on in, I'm going to assume that you have the former and are working on the latter. You're a good person, especially because you bought this book.

Icons Used in This Book

Scattered throughout the book are little pictures, which my publisher calls icons, in the margins next to certain blocks of text. Here's what they mean:

This icon lets you know that I'm presenting a neat hint or trick that can make your life easier.

This icon flags information that will keep you out of trouble.

Where to Go from Here

You've got your minibook copy of *Cocktails For Dummies, Pocket Edition* — now what? This minibook is a reference, so if you're brand new to the art of bartending, think about reading Chapter 1 first — it's meant just for you and includes a lot of pointers about the equipment and glasses you'll need. Like those little garnishes? Chapter 2 is exactly what you need. Or if you're ready to start mixing, head on over to Chapter 3.

When it comes to the recipes, I do have this bit of advice: I recommend that you use only the best ingredients when making cocktails. They represent your opinion of your guests, and you want them to have the best. In some drinks, you can get by with the cheap stuff, but in this day and age, people are drinking less and demanding higher quality. You can't go wrong when you serve the good stuff, so why serve anything else?

If you want even more recipes or want info on the different types of liquers, check out the full-size version of *Bartending For Dummies,* 3rd Edition — simply head to your local book seller or go to `www.dummies.com`!

That said, get reading and start pouring.

Chapter 1

Just for Openers: The Right Tools and Glasses

In This Chapter

- All the bartending tools you need
- More glasses than you can shake a drink at

To bartend, you need a few essentials: You need to have good people skills and to know about the products that you're pouring; cocktail recipes and proper equipment are also necessary. This chapter covers equipment.

The Basic Tools

The most important assets for any profession are the right tools. You need basic bar tools to mix, serve, and store your drinks. Whether you're stocking a home bar or working as a professional, your basic tools are a wine opener, cocktail shaker, measuring glass, and strainer.

Wine opener

The best wine opener is a waiter's wine opener (shown in Figure 1-1). It has a sharp blade, a corkscrew (also known as a worm), and a bottle opener. This wine opener can be found in most liquor stores or bar supply houses.

Another nifty wine opener is called a Rabbit. It's also shown in Figure 1-1.

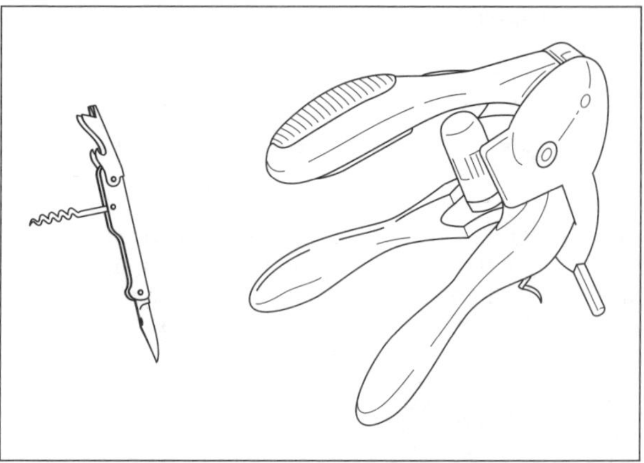

Figure 1-1: A waiter's wine opener and a Rabbit.

Cocktail shaker

Figure 1-2 shows two types of shakers. The Boston shaker is the one that most professional bartenders use. It consists of a mixing glass and a stainless steel core that overlaps the glass. The Standard shaker usually consists of two or more stainless steel or glass parts and can be found in department stores or antiques stores. Many of these shakers come in different shapes and designs.

Figure 1-2: A Boston shaker and a Standard shaker.

Strainer

A couple of different types of strainers are available, but the most popular is the Hawthorn, shown in Figure 1-3.

The Hawthorn is a flat, spoon-shaped utensil with a spring coil around its head. You can use it on top of a steel shaker or a bar glass to strain cocktails.

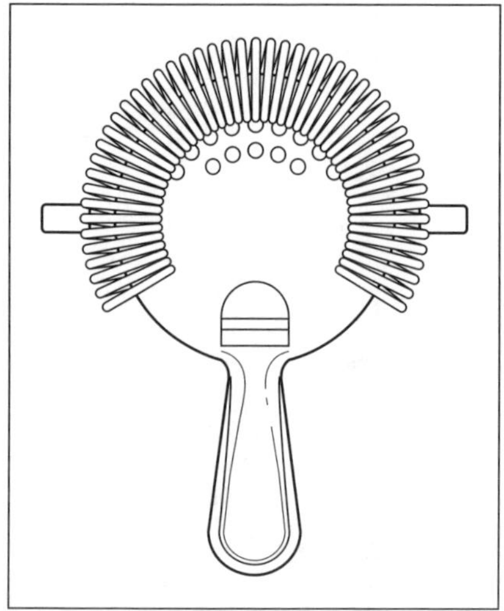

Figure 1-3: The Hawthorn strainer.

Other tools

Many of the following tools are shown in Figure 1-4:

- **Bar spoon:** A long spoon for stirring cocktails.
- **Blender:** Many types of commercial or home blenders with various speeds are available. When making a drink, always put liquid in the blender before switching it on. This will save your blade.

Some blenders (but not all) can be used to make crushed ice. Check with the manufacturer or buy an ice crusher.

- **Coasters or bar napkins:** Coasters prevent rings from developing on your bar and other tables. Napkins also help your guests hold their drinks.
- **Ice bucket:** Pick one that's large enough to hold at least three trays of ice.
- **Ice scoop or tongs:** A must for every bar. Never use your hands to scoop ice.
- **Jigger or measuring glass:** A small glass or metal measuring container that usually has a ½ oz. measurer on one side and a 2 oz. measurer on the other.
- **Knife and cutting board:** You need a small, sharp paring knife to cut fruit.
- **Large water pitcher:** Someone always wants water.
- **Muddler:** A small wooden bat or pestle used to crush fruit or herbs.
- **Pourer:** This device gives greater control to your pouring. A variety of different types is available, including some with a lidded spout, which prevents insects and undesirables from entering the pourer.
- **Stirrers and straws:** Used for stirring and sipping drinks.
- **Large cups or bowls:** Used to hold garnishes, such as cherries, olives, onions, and so on.

Figure 1-4: A collection of bar tools: (1) bar spoon, (2) blender, (3) tongs, (4) ice scoop, (5) ice bucket, (6) jigger or measuring glass, (7) knife and cutting board, (8) muddler, and (9) pourer.

Glassware

People generally expect certain drinks to be served in certain kinds of glasses. The problem is that there are more standard bar glasses than most people (and many bars) care to purchase. In any event, Figures 1-5 and 1-6 show most of the glasses that you're ever likely to use to serve drinks.

I have a few things to say about some of the glasses shown:

- **Shot glass:** You can also use the shot glass as a measuring tool. It's a must for every bar.
- **Cocktail or martini glass:** Perfect for martinis, Manhattans, stingers, and many other classic drinks, this glass is available in 3 to 6 oz. sizes.
- **White wine glass:** This glass is available in 5 to 10 oz. sizes. I advise you to stick with the smaller wine glass.
- **Red wine glass:** This glass is also available in 5 to 10 oz. sizes. Note that the bowl is wider than the bowl of a white wine glass, allowing the wine to breathe.
- **Champagne glass:** The bowl is tapered to prevent bubbles from escaping.
- **Rocks glass:** Also known as an old-fashioned glass, sizes vary from 5 to 10 oz. Use the 5 or 6 oz. variety and add plenty of ice.
- **Highball and Collins glasses:** These glasses are the most versatile. Sizes range from 8 to 12 oz.
- **Cordial glass:** In addition to cordials, you can also use this glass to serve straight-up drinks.
- **Brandy or cognac snifter:** Available in a wide range of sizes, the short stemmed, large bowl should be cupped in hand to warm the brandy or cognac.
- **Stemless glasses:** These glasses have become popular in recent years, probably because they look elegant even if they aren't as practical as the stemmed versions.

If you're planning on creating a bar at home or serving cocktails at a party, keep your glass selection small. You can simplify by using two types of glasses: a white wine glass and a red wine glass. Both are shown in Figure 1-6. These two glasses can be used for every type of cocktail (including shots, even though I said that a shot glass is essential for every bar) plus beer and wine. Also, if you use these two glass shapes, cleaning and storing your glasses is less complicated.

Figure 1-5: Glasses, glasses, glasses.

Figure 1-6: More glasses.

Chapter 2

Methods to the Madness

In This Chapter

- Prepping some great garnishes
- Mixing it up with style
- Popping the champagne
- Conjuring up some bar syrup

Making good cocktails takes more effort than just pouring ingredients into a glass. This chapter shows you how to pull off some of the little touches that make both you and your drinks look better, with the ultimate result of happier guests.

Cutting Fruit

Many drinks require fruit garnishes. Your guests expect the garnish, so you can't forgo it, and you have to do it well. Presentation counts big time. You may mix the best drinks on the planet, but if they don't look good when you serve them, no one's going to want to drink them.

I've stepped away from the pulpit now. The next few diagrams and steps show you how to cut the most common garnishes.

Lemon twists

Figure 2-1 illustrates the procedure for cutting lemon twists.

1. **Cut off both ends of the lemon.**
2. **Insert a sharp knife or spoon between the rind and meat of the lemon and carefully separate them.**
3. **Cut the rind into strips.**

The outside of the lemon is where the flavor lies. When adding a lemon twist to a drink, slowly rim the edge of the glass with the outside of the lemon twist and then twist a drop into the cocktail.

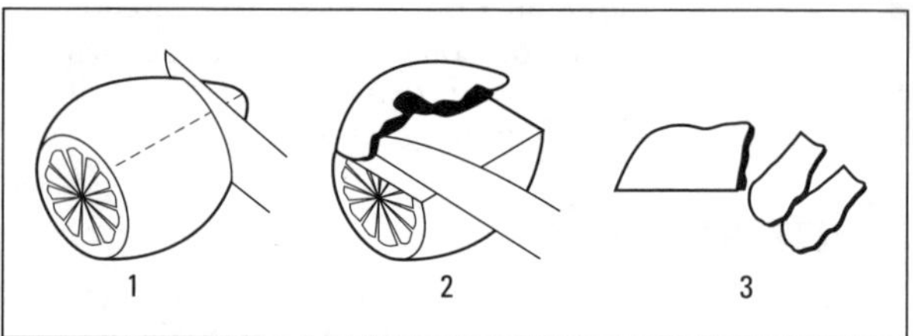

Figure 2-1: Cutting lemon twists.

Orange slices

The following steps for cutting orange slices are shown in Figure 2-2.

1. **With the ends of the orange removed, cut the orange in half.**
2. **Cut each half in half again (lengthwise).**
3. **Cut the orange quarters into wedges.**

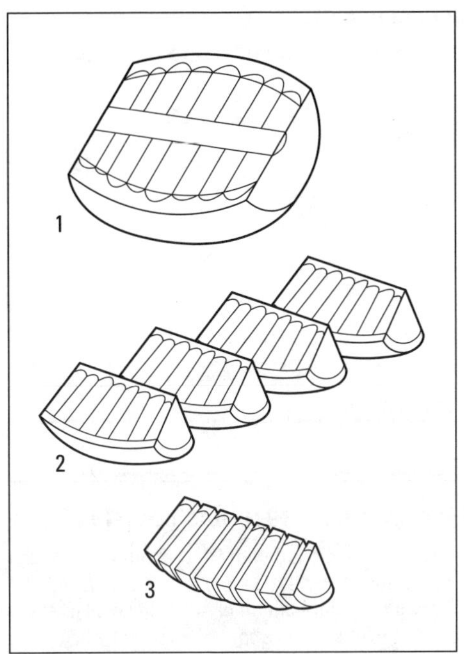

Figure 2-2: Cutting orange slices.

Lime slices

The next few steps and Figure 2-3 show you how to cut lime slices.

1. **Cut off both ends of the lime.**
2. **Slice the lime in half.**
3. **Lay each half down and cut it into half-moon slices.**

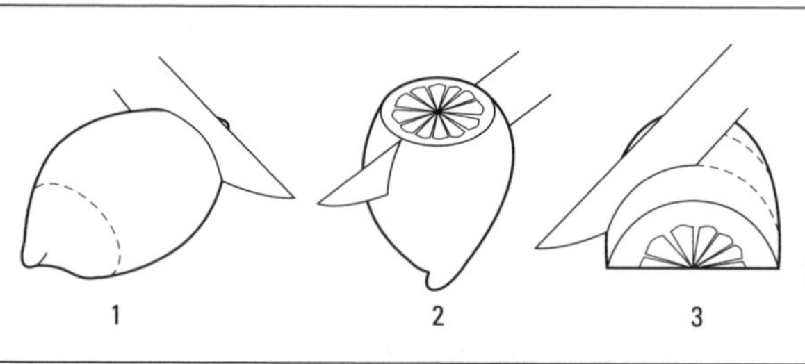

Figure 2-3: Cutting lime slices.

Don't forget the Maraschino cherries

All kinds of drinks are garnished with Maraschino cherries, including the kid-friendly Shirley Temple and the more adult Manhattan. You can find Maraschino cherries in small jars at any food store, and the best thing about them is that you don't have to cut them before serving.

Lemon and lime wedges

Figure 2-4 illustrates the following steps for cutting wedges.

1. **Slice the lemon or lime in half the long way.**
2. **Lay the cut halves down and halve them again.**
3. **Cut wedges from the lemon or lime quarters.**

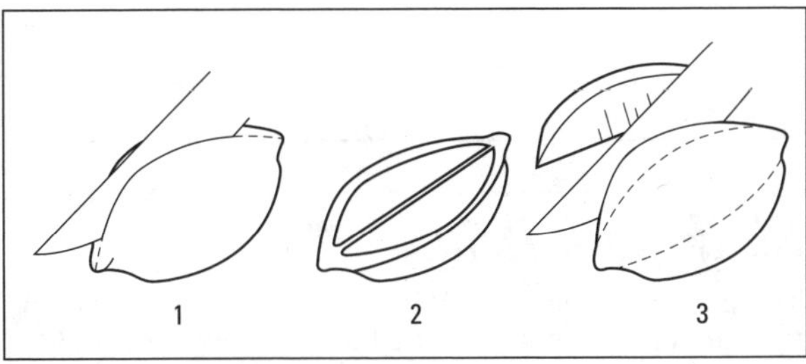

Figure 2-4: Cutting lemon or lime wedges.

Pineapple wedges

Figure 2-5 and the following steps show you how to cut pineapple wedges.

1. **Cut off the top and bottom of the pineapple.**
2. **From top to bottom, cut the pineapple in half.**
3. **Lay the half pineapple down and cut it in half again.**
4. **Remove the core section of the pineapple quarters.**
5. **Cut wedges.**

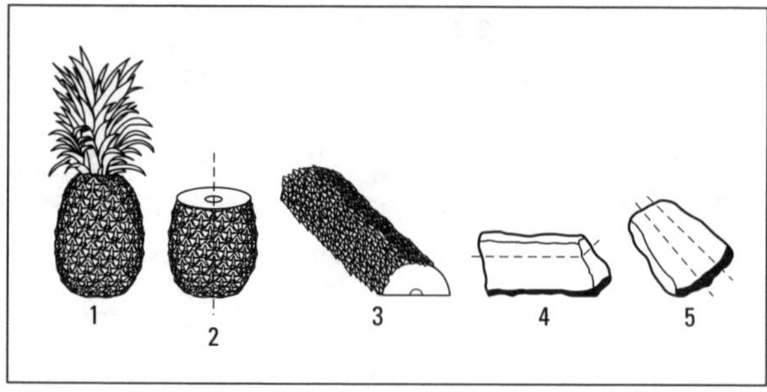

Figure 2-5: Cutting pineapple wedges.

Shaking a Drink

The main reasons for shaking drinks are to chill a cocktail, mix ingredients, or put a head on some cocktails.

As a general rule, you should shake all cloudy drinks (including cream drinks and sours), and you should stir all clear drinks. Never shake a cocktail that has carbonated water or soda. For some drinks, such as the stinger or martini, ask your guests whether they prefer them shaken or stirred.

To shake a cocktail in a Boston shaker, follow these steps:

1. **Put some ice cubes (if called for in the recipe) in the glass container.**
2. **Add the cocktail ingredients.**

3. **Place the metal container over the glass container.**
4. **Hold the metal and glass containers together with both hands and shake with an up and down motion.**

Make sure that you always point the shaker away from your guests. This way you avoid spilling anything on them if the shaker isn't properly sealed.

The two pieces of the shaker may stick together after you shake a drink. Never bang the shaker against the bar or any other object; instead, gently tap it three or four times at the point where the glass and metal containers come in contact.

When pouring or straining the cocktail, always pour from the glass container.

Opening Wine and Champagne Bottles

Opening bottles doesn't take much skill, just a little practice. It's a no-brainer task, so if you don't get it right, you'll look like a fool.

Wine bottles

To open a wine bottle, you want to use a waiter's opener, which I show you in Chapter 1. Then go through these numbered steps:

1. **Using the blade on the opener, cut the lead foil or capsule at the middle of the bulge near the bottle neck.**

2. **Remove the foil and wipe the bottle top with a cloth to remove any mold or foreign particles.**
3. **Line up the screw or worm directly over the bottle, and with gentle downward pressure, screw the worm clockwise into the cork.**

   Don't break the end of the cork, and screw in just enough to extract the cork.
4. **Attach the lever of the opener to the lip on top of the bottle, and while holding the bottle firmly, slowly lift the cork straight up.**
5. **Wipe the neck of the bottle.**
6. **Present the cork to your guest and pour one ounce of wine into his or her glass.**

If the wine is to your guest's satisfaction, pour more. Keep your towel handy to wipe the neck of the bottle as you pour the wine for other guests.

Champagne and sparkling wine bottles

You don't use a corkscrew when opening sparkling wine bottles.

1. **Remove the wine hood and foil capsule.**
2. **Hold the bottle at an angle and point it away from you and anyone else (and anything valuable).**
3. **While holding the cork in one hand, twist the bottle with the other hand and gently remove the cork. Remember, twist the bottle, not the cork.**

4. **Just before the cork is about to pop, place a bar towel over the cork and bottle and loosen it the rest of the way. (The towel will catch the cork and prevent the cork from becoming a UFO.)**

Keep another towel handy in case the bottle bubbles over after you remove the cork. To avoid the bubbling, don't shake the bottle before opening.

Making Simple Syrup

Several cocktail recipes call for simple syrup. To make it, dissolve one part sugar in one part boiling water and reduce the mixture over low heat, stirring frequently, until it thickens. It shouldn't take more than a couple minutes.

Chapter 3

Recipes from A to Z

In This Chapter

- Many, many cocktail recipes
- A few stories to keep things interesting

You probably bought this book just for the recipes. Some are classic drinks that you've probably heard of; others are new and trendy. Most are quite good; some are strange concoctions that few people like.

One final note: Just in case you don't know, the term *straight up* means without ice.

A Tinker Tall

1¼ oz. Irish Mist
3 oz. Ginger Ale
3 oz. Club Soda

Combine ingredients with lots of ice in a tall glass.

The After Ten

1 part Galliano
1 part Remy Martin Cognac

Rim glass with brown sugar. Add freshly brewed coffee and top with whipped cream.

Alice in Wonderland

1 part Herradura Tequila
1 part Tia Maria
1 part Grand Marnier

Shake with ice and strain into shot glass.

This one will get the cast smiling.

Americano

1 oz. Martini & Rossi Rosso Vermouth
1 oz. Campari
Club soda

Build with ice in a highball glass.Top with Club Soda and a twist.

A classic from Italy.

Apple Kir

1 oz. Jose Cuervo Gold Tequila
½ oz. Crème de Cassis
1 oz. Apple Juice
1 tsp. Fresh Lemon Juice

Mix in a rocks glass over ice. Garnish with a Lemon Wedge.

Apricot Sour

2 Tbsp. Lemon Juice
½ tsp. Superfine Sugar
2 oz. Apricot Brandy
3-4 Ice Cubes

Combine all ingredients in a shaker and shake vigorously. Strain into a chilled cocktail glass. Garnish with Lemon.

The hot drink of the 60s.

B-52

1 part Grand Marnier
1 part Kahlua
1 part Baileys Irish Cream

Shake with ice. Strain or serve over ice.

You can also serve this one as a shot.

B&B

1 oz. Benedictine
1 oz. Brandy

Stir and serve in a snifter.

An easy one to remember.

Bacardi & Tonic

1¼ oz. Bacardi Light Rum
Tonic

Pour Rum into a tall glass filled with ice. Fill with Tonic.

A change in mixer.

Bagpiper

1½ oz. 100 Pipers Scotch
3 oz. Coffee

Stir in an Irish coffee glass and top with whipped cream.

Baileys French Dream

1½ oz. Baileys Irish Cream
½ oz. Raspberry Liqueur
2 oz. Half & Half
4 oz. Ice Cubes

Blend for 30 seconds and serve.

Bamboo Cocktail

1½ oz. Sherry
¾ oz. Dry Vermouth
dash Angostura Bitters

Stir with ice and strain.

This drink was invented around 1910 by bartender Charlie Mahoney of the Hoffman House in New York, New York.

Barracuda

1¼ oz. Ronrico Dark Rum
1 oz. Pineapple Juice
½ oz. Rose's Lime Juice
¼ tsp. Sugar
Champagne

Shake everything but the Champagne. Serve in a champagne glass and fill to the top with Champagne.

Bellini

1 Peach Half
Champagne
Simple Syrup

Muddle the Peach in a champagne glass with a little Simple Syrup. Fill the glass with Champagne.

Invented at Harry's Bar in Venice, Italy, by Giuseppi Cipriani on the occasion of an exhibition of the work of Venetian painter Bellini.

Black Buck

1¼ oz. Bacardi Black Rum
Ginger Ale

Pour Rum in a tall glass with ice. Fill with Ginger Ale and garnish with Lemon.

Black Martini

1½ oz. Absolut Kurant
splash Chambord

Stir ingredients and serve straight up or over ice.

Invented at the Continental Cafe in Philadelphia, Pennsylvania.

Black Tie Martini

1½ oz. Skyy Vodka
Splash Campari
Splash Chivas
2 Cocktail Onions
1 Black Olive

Shake with ice and strain into chilled martini glass.

Bloody Mary

1¼ oz. Vodka
2½ oz. Tomato Juice
dash Worcestershire Sauce
dash Tabasco Sauce
dash Salt and Pepper

Pour Vodka over ice in a glass. Fill with Tomato Juice. Add a dash or two of Worcestershire Sauce and Tabasco Sauce.Stir and garnish with a Celery Stalk. For those who enjoy their Bloody Marys extremely spicy, add more Tabasco or even Horseradish.

The most famous of the "Hair of the Dog" morning-after cocktails.

Blue Blazer

2 parts Irish Whiskey
1 part Clear Honey
½ part Lemon Juice
1–3 parts Water

Pour all ingredients into a pan and heat very gently until the Honey has dissolved. Place a teaspoon into a short tumbler and pour drink carefully into the glass (the spoon keeps the glass from cracking). Serve with Cinnamon Sticks.

Bolero

1½ oz. Rhum Barbancort
½ oz. Calvados
2 tsp. Sweet Vermouth
dash Bitters

Stir. Serve straight up or with ice.

You can also serve this drink as a shot.

Brain

1 oz. Baileys Irish Cream
1 oz. Peach or Strawberry Schnapps

Serve straight up in a shot glass.

This will keep you thinking.

Bushmills Fuzzy Valencia

1½ oz. Bushmills Irish Whiskey
¾ oz. Amaretto
5 oz. Orange Juice

Serve in a tall glass over ice.

Buttery Nipple

⅓ oz. Irish Cream
⅓ oz. Vodka
⅓ oz. Butterscotch Schnapps

Combine in a shot glass.

Cannonball

1½ oz. Captain Morgan Spiced Rum
3 oz. Pineapple Juice
¼ oz. White Crème de Menthe

Pour the Rum and Pineapple Juice over ice. Float the Crème de Menthe on top.

Big noise in a rocks glass.

Caribbean Joy

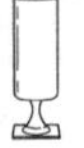

1¼ oz. Castillo Silver Rum
1 oz. Pineapple Juice
¾ oz. Lemon Juice

Shake and serve over ice.

Champerelle

1 part Orange Curacao
1 part Anisette
1 part Green Chartreuse
1 part Cognac

Layer this drink in the order listed. Start with Orange Curacao on the bottom and finish with Cognac on top.

Chicago Style

¾ oz. Bacardi Light Rum
¼ oz. Hiram Walker Triple Sec
¼ oz. Hiram Walker Anisette
¼ oz. Lemon or Lime Juice

Blend with ice.

The windy one.

Chocolate Martini #1

1 oz. Absolut Vodka
½ oz. Godiva Chocolate Liqueur

Shake over ice; strain into a chilled cocktail glass with a Lemon Twist garnish.

For your sweet tooth.

Cilver Citron

1¼ oz. Absolut Citron
2 oz. Chilled Champagne

Combine in a champagne glass.

Citron Kamikazi

¾ oz. Absolut Citron Vodka
¾ oz. Triple Sec
Lime Juice

Pour Citron, Triple Sec, and Lime Juice over ice in a glass. Shake well and strain into a glass. Serve straight up or over ice. Garnish with a Lime Wedge.

Coco Loco (Crazy Coconut)

1½ oz. Herradura Tequila
3 oz. Pineapple Juice
2 oz. Coco Lopez Cream of Coconut

Blend. Garnish with a Pineapple Spear.

Cool Mist

2 oz. Irish Mist
Tonic Water

Combine in a tall glass with crushed ice. Add a Shamrock for a garnish.

Cosmopolitan Martini

1 part Cointreau
2 parts Vodka
Juice of ½ Lime
splash Cranberry

Shake with ice and strain.

There are many variations of the martini. This one works.

Cran Razz

2 oz. Two Fingers Tequila
2 oz. Cranberry Juice
1 oz. Raspberry Liqueur

In a shaker, mix all ingredients. Serve over ice.

Creature from the Black Lagoon

1 oz. Jagermeister
1 oz. Romana Black

Shake with ice and strain into a shot glass.

Back to the water.

Cuba Libre

1¾ oz. Bacardi Rum
Cola
Juice of ¼ Lime

Add Rum to a glass filled with ice. Fill with Cola. Add Lime Juice and stir.

A Rum and cola with a lime.

Daiquiri

1¼ oz. Light Rum
½ oz. Sweetened Lemon Juice

Shake or blend with ice.

Cuba Libre Lore

This drink is a political statement as well as a cocktail. It translates to Free Cuba, a status that the country enjoyed in 1898 at the end of the Spanish-American War. Cuban-American relations were friendly around the turn of the century, when a U.S. Army lieutenant in Havana mixed some light native rum with a new-fangled American soft drink called Coca-Cola and braced the libation with a lime.

Dark 'N Stormy

1½ oz. Gosling's Black Seal Rum
4 oz. Ginger Beer

Pour the Rum over ice and top with Ginger Beer. Garnish with Lime or Lemon Wedge (optional).

Bermuda's national drink.

Dean Martini

2 oz. Ketel One Vodka, chilled
Olive
1 Lucky (cigarette)
1 book of matches

Pour the Vodka into a cocktail glass and garnish with an Olive. Place the Cigarette and Matches on the side.

Invented at the Continental Cafe in Philadelphia, Pennsylvania.

Dirty Harry

1 oz. Grand Marnier
1 oz. Tia Maria

Shake with ice and strain.

Do you feel lucky? This will make your day.

Dubonnet Cocktail

1½ oz. Dubonnet
½ oz. Gin
dash Angostura Bitters

Combine over ice and garnish with a Lemon Twist.

Egg Nog

1¼ oz. Bacardi Light or Dark Rum
1 Egg
1 tsp. Sugar
1 oz. Milk

Mix in a shaker and strain into a glass. Sprinkle with Nutmeg.

Erie Tour

1 part Irish Mist
1 part Carolans Irish Cream
1 part Irish Whiskey

Combine over ice.

Fifty-Fifty

1½ oz. Gin
1½ oz. Vermouth

Stir ingredients over ice in a shaker and strain into a chilled martini glass. Garnish with an olive.

A very wet martini.

Firebird

1¼ oz. Absolut Peppar Vodka
4 oz. Cranberry Juice

Combine over ice.

Fools Gold

1 part Vodka
1 part Galliano

Shake with ice and strain into a shot glass.

French Connection

½ oz. Cognac
½ oz. Grand Marnier

Serve straight up in a brandy snifter or shake with ice and strain.

You can also serve this drink as a shot.

Fudgesicle

1 oz. Vodka
¼ oz. Crème de Cacao
¼ oz. Chocolate Syrup

Shake and serve over ice.

German Chocolate Cake

1 oz. Malibu Rum
½ oz. Creme de Cacao
½oz. Frangelico
½ oz. Half & Half

Shake with ice. Pour over rocks or serve straight up.

Gimlet

1¼ oz. Vodka
½ oz. Fresh Lime Juice

Mix Vodka and Lime Juice in a glass with ice. Strain and serve in a cocktail glass. Garnish with a Lime Twist.

You can also serve this one on ice in a highball glass.

Gin & Tonic

1¼ oz. Gin
Tonic

In a glass fllled with ice, add Gin and fill with Tonic. Add a Lime Wedge.

Godmother

1 oz. Vodka
¼ oz. Amaretto

Combine in a rocks glass over ice.

A woman you can't refuse.

Good and Plenty

1 oz. Anisette
1 oz. Blackberry Brandy

Shake with ice and strain into a shot glass.

Green Hornet

½ oz. Vodka ¼ oz. Midori ½ oz. Sweet & Sour Mix	Shake with ice; serve straight up or over ice.

Harry's Martini

1¾ oz. Dry Gin ¾ oz. Sweet Vermouth ¼ oz. Pernod	Stir gently with ice; serve straight up or on ice. Garnish with Mint Sprigs.

Harvard Cocktail

1½ oz. Brandy ¾ oz. Sweet Vermouth 2 tsp. Fresh Lemon Juice 1 tsp. Grenadine dash Angostura Bitters	Shake ingredients and serve over ice in a rocks glass.

Hawaii Five-O

1½ oz. Finlandia Pineapple Vodka ¼ oz. Blue Curacao	Shake. Serve in a glass with ice. Garnish with a Pineapple Spear, Cherry, and umbrella.

Highball

1½ oz. American Whiskey 3 oz. Ginger Ale	Combine and stir.

Hot Mist

2 parts Irish Mist 1 part Boiling Water	Combine in the glass and garnish with a slice of Lemon and some Cloves.

Incredible Hulk

2 oz. Hpnotiq
2 oz. Cognac

Layer over ice and then stir for transformation.

Innisfree Fizz

2 oz. Irish Whiskey
1 oz. Lemon Juice
1 oz. Orange Curacao
½ oz. Sugar Syrup
Club Soda

Mix all ingredients except Club Soda with cracked ice in a shaker or blender. Strain into a chilled wine goblet and fill with Club Soda.

Irish Buck

1½ oz. Irish Whiskey
Ginger Ale

Pour Irish Whiskey into chilled highball glass with cracked ice. Twist a Lemon Peel over the drink and drop it in. Fill with Ginger Ale.

Irish Headlock

¼ oz. Brandy
¼ oz. Amaretto
¼ oz. Irish Whiskey
¼ oz. Irish Cream

Layer this drink by pouring the Brandy first, then the Amaretto, and so on.

Irish Summer Coffee

1 oz. Irish Whiskey
¼ oz. Irish Cream Liqueur
4 oz. Cold Coffee
Whipped Cream

Stir first three ingredients with ice and strain. Top with Whipped Cream if desired.

Irish Whiskey Sour

1 jigger Irish Whiskey
1 bar spoon Sugar
Juice of 1 Lemon

Shake ingredients with ice and strain. Garnish with an Orange Slice and a Cherry.

Italian Russian

½ oz. Sambuca
1 oz. Vodka

Pour over ice cubes in small rocks glass. Stir well. Twist an Orange Peel over the glass and drop it in.

James Bond Martini #1

3 parts Gordon's Gin
1 part Vodka
½ part Kina Lillet

Shake ingredients with ice until very cold. Pour into a chilled glass. Then add a large, thin slice of Lemon Peel.

From the 1967 movie Casino Royale.

Jamie's Highland Special

1 part Green Crème de Menthe
1 part Galliano
1 part Blackberry Liqueur
1 part Kirschwasser

Layer this drink in the order listed. Start with Crème de Menthe on the bottom and finish with Kirschwasser on top.

Jolly Rancher #1

¾ oz. Peach Schnapps
¾ oz. Apple Schnapps
2½ oz. Cranberry Juice

Combine in a tall glass with ice.

Jump Up and Kiss Me

1¼ oz. Myers's Dark Rum
4 oz. Pineapple Juice
½ oz. Rose's Lime Juice
dash Angostura

Shake with ice and serve over ice.

Kahlua Sunset

1 oz. Kahlua
2½ oz. Cranberry Juice
3 oz. Pineapple Juice

Combine in a tall glass with ice.

Kamikazi

1 oz. Vodka
½ oz. Cointreau
¼ oz. Rose's Lime Juice

Shake with ice and strain into a shot glass.

Killer Colada

2 oz. Whaler's Coconut Rum
3 Tbsp. Coconut Milk
3 Tbsp. Pineapple (crushed)
2 cups Crushed Ice

Blend at high speed. Serve with a Pineapple Wedge.

Kir or Kir Royale

3 oz. Champagne
splash Crème de Cassis

Fill the glass with Champagne and add a splash of Crème de Cassis.

Latin Lover

1 oz. Herradura Tequila
½ oz. Amaretto

Combine in a rocks glass over ice.

You can also serve this one as a shot (without the ice).

Lazer Beam

1 part Bourbon
1 part Rumple Minze
1 part Drambuie

Shake with ice and strain into a shot glass.

Leprechaun

1½ oz. Irish Whiskey
3 oz. Tonic Water
3–4 Ice Cubes

Put Whiskey and Tonic Water in a rocks glass. Add Ice Cubes and stir gently. Drop in a slice of Lemon Peel.

Long Island Iced Tea

½ oz. Vodka
½ oz. Rum
½ oz. Gin
½ oz. Triple Sec
½ oz. Tequila
Cola

Shake the first five ingredients over ice and strain into a glass. Fill with Cola.

There are many variations on this popular drink.

What twisted genius created Long Island Iced Tea?

This drink does hail from Long Island, specifically the Oak Beach Inn in Hampton Bays. Spirits writer John Mariani credits bartender Robert (Rosebud) Butt as the inventor, whose original recipe called for an ounce each of clear liquors (vodka, gin, tequila, light rum), a half ounce of triple sec, some lemon juice, and a splash of cola.

This drink comes in many forms and is still popular with young drinkers, though not with those who have to get up early the next day.

Maiden's Prayer

2 parts Cork Dry Gin
2 parts Cointreau
1 part Orange Juice
1 part Lemon Juice

Shake with ice and strain into a glass.

Mai Tai

¾ oz. Bacardi Light Rum
¼ oz. Bacardi 151 Rum
½ oz. Orange Curacao
½ oz. Rose's Lime Juice
¼ oz. Orgeat Syrup
¼ oz. Simple Syrup

Stir with ice. Garnish with Mint, Cherry, and Pineapple.

Mai Tai: Out of this world

Vic Bergeron invented the Mai Tai in 1944 at his Polynesian-style Oakland bar. He didn't want fruit juices detracting from the two ounces of J. Wray Nephew Jamaican rum he poured as the base for his creation. He merely added a half ounce of French orgeat (an almond-flavored syrup), a half ounce of orange curacao, a quarter ounce of rock candy syrup, and the juice of one lime. Customer Carrie Wright of Tahiti, the first to taste the concoction, responded, "Mai tai . . . roe ae!" (Tahitian for "Out of this world . . . the best!")

The Mai Tai became famous, and conflicting stories about its origins aggravated Bergeron so much that he elicited a sworn statement from Mrs. Wright in 1970, testifying to his authorship of the cocktail.

Malibu Beach

1½ oz. Malibu
1 oz. Smirnoff Vodka
4 oz. Orange Juice

Combine over ice.

Manhattan

2 oz. American or Canadian Whisky
splash Sweet or Dry Vermouth
dash Angostura Bitters

Stir. Garnish with a Cherry.

Melon Ball

¾ oz. Midori
1 oz. Vodka
4 oz. Orange Juice

Combine in a glass and stir.

Mexico Martini

1½ oz. Gran Centenario Plata Tequila
1 tbsp. Extra Dry Vermouth
2–3 drops Vanilla Extract

Shake and strain into an iced glass.

Manhattan

The Manhattan recipe was created around 1874 at the Manhattan Club, New York, for Lady Randolph Churchill, Winston's mother. She was attending a banquet in honor of the lawyer and politician Samuel J. Tilden at the time.

Midnight Martini

1½ oz. Vodka
½ oz. Chambord

Stir with ice and strain.
Garnish with a Lemon Twist.

From the Gallery Lounge Sheraton in Seattle, Washington.

Martini mythology

You're likely to hear several stories about the creation of the martini, such as the few that follow:

- A stranger on his way to Martinez, California, told bartender Jerry Thomas of San Francisco, California, about this drink made with gin, vermouth, bitters, and dash of maraschino.
- A bartender in Martinez, California, created it for a gold-miner who struck it rich: The miner ordered champagne for the house, but none was available. The bartender offered something better — a Martinez Special — some sauterne and gin. The rich miner spread the word throughout California about this Martinez Special.
- The drink is named after Martini & Rossi vermouth because it was first used in the drink, Gin and It, which contains Gin and Martini & Rossi vermouth.
- The drink is named after the British army rifle, the Martini and Henry. The rifle was known for its kick, like the first sip of Gin and It.
- At the Knickerbocker Hotel in the early 1900s, a bartender named Martini di Arma Tiggia mixed a martini using only a dry gin and dry vermouth.

Mimosa

3 oz. Champagne
2 oz. Orange Juice

Combine in a champagne flute and stir.

A great brunch drink.

Mist Old Fashioned

1¼ oz. Irish Mist
Orange Slice
Cherry Bitters
Sugar
Club Soda or Water

Muddle the Orange, Cherry Bitters, and Sugar. Add Irish Mist. Top with Club Soda or Water.

Mistic Beach

1¼ oz. Jose Cuervo Mistico
¾ oz. Cointreau
3 oz. Cranberry Juice

Combine over ice in a tall glass. Stir. Garnish with a Lemon Wedge.

Mojito

2 oz. Bacardi Light Rum
8 Mint Leaves
Juice of ½ Lime
2 tsp. Sugar
4 oz. Club Soda

In a Collins glass, place Mint Leaves and Lime Juice, crush with a muddler or the back of a spoon, and add Sugar. Fill glass with ice, add Rum, and top with Club Soda. Stir well and garnish with a sprig of Mint.

The Mimosa: A French creation

The Mimosa was created around 1925 at the Ritz Hotel Bar in Paris, France. It took its name from the mimosa flowering plant, whose color it resembles.

Monsoon

¼ oz. Vodka
¼ oz. Coffee Liqueur
¼ oz. Amaretto
¼ oz. Irish Cream
¼ oz. Hazelnut Liqueur

Shake with ice; serve over ice.

Moscow Mule

1½ oz. Smirnoff Vodka
4 oz. Ginger Beer

Stir with ice. Garnish with a Lime Wedge.

Should be served in a bronze cup or mug.

Ms. Tea

1¼ oz. Irish Mist
3 oz. Iced Tea

Mix with ice; serve over ice.

Myers's Strawberry Daiquiri

1¼ oz. Myers's Dark Rum
½ oz. Triple Sec
Juice of ½ Lime
½ cup Strawberries
1 tsp. Bar Sugar

Blend with crushed ice.

Negroni

½ oz. Dry Vermouth ½ oz. Bombay Gin ½ oz. Campari	Combine in a rocks glass over ice.

Neon Tequila Monster

1 oz. Burnett's Vodka 1 oz. Tequila 3 oz. Orange Juice	Combine over ice.

Nervous Breakdown

1½ oz. Vodka ½ oz. Chambord splash Cranberry Juice Soda	Combine the first three ingredients in a tall glass. Fill with Soda.

Neva

1½ oz. Vodka ½ oz. Tomato Juice ½ oz. Orange Juice	In a shaker, mix all ingredients. Pour over ice into a stemmed glass.

Nuts & Berrys

½ oz. Vodka ½ oz. Hazelnut Liqueur ½ oz. Coffee Liqueur ¼ oz. Cream	Combine with ice and shake. Strain and serve straight up in a rocks glass.

O.J. Mist

1 part Irish Mist 3 parts Orange Juice	Combine in a tall glass over ice.

Oil Slick

1 part Rumple Minze
1 part Bourbon

Shake with ice and strain into a shot glass.

Old San Juan

Lime Wedge
1½ oz. Gold Rum
½ oz. Cranberry Juice
1 oz. Fresh Lime Juice

Rim a chilled martini glass with the Lime Wedge. Combine other ingredients in cocktail shaker with ice. Shake well and strain into the glass. Squeeze Lime Wedge into the drink and drop it in.

Oyster Shooter

1 oz. Vodka
1 Raw Oyster
1 tsp. Cocktail Sauce

Pour Vodka over the Oyster and Sauce in a small rocks glass and stir. Add a squeeze of Lemon.

You can also add a dash of horseradish if you dare.

Parisian Pousse-Café

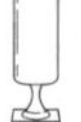

2 parts Orange Curacao
2 parts Kirschwasser
1 part Chartreuse

Layer this drink in the order listed. Start with Curacao on the bottom and finish with Chartreuse on top.

Pearl Diver

1½ oz. Midori
½ oz. Coconut Rum
4 oz. Orange Juice

Combine in a tall glass over ice.

Picadilly

2 parts Cork Dry Gin
1 part Dry Vermouth
dash Pernod
dash Grenadine

Mix with ice. Serve over ice.

Pink Gin (a.k.a. Gin & Bitters)

1¾ oz. Gin
dash Angostura Bitters

Rinse a chilled glass with Bitters. Add Gin.

Poet's Punch

1 oz. Irish Mist
1 stick Cinnamon
twist Lemon
twist Orange
½ tsp. Vanilla
½ cup Milk

Heat the Milk, Cinnamon Stick, and Lemon and Orange Twists to boiling point. Add Vanilla and Irish Mist. Strain. Sprinkle with Nutmeg.

The ori-gins of Pink Gin

In 1824, Dr. Johan G. B. Siegert created Angostura bitters as a remedy for stomach complaints suffered by the Venezuelan army. He named this concoction after the town on the Orinoco River where he had worked.

The British Navy added this product to its medicine chest but soon discovered that it added a whole new dimension to Plymouth gin, and thus Pink Gin came to be.

Purple Hooter Martini

1¼ oz. Chambord
1¼ oz. Vodka
¼ oz. Sour Mix
¼ oz. Lemon-Lime Soda

Combine ingredients, except Soda, into shaker filled with ice. Shake thoroughly and pour into martini glass. Top with Lemon-Lime Soda.

Purple Passion

1¼ oz. Vodka
2 oz. Grapefruit Juice
2 oz. Grape Juice

Combine ingredients and stir. Chill and add Sugar to taste. Serve in a collins glass.

Raspberripolitan

2 oz. Absolut Raspberri
½ oz. Cointreau
½ oz. Cranberry Juice
1 dash Lime Juice
Lime Wedge

Shake with ice and strain into a well-chilled cocktail glass. Garnish with a Lime Wedge.

A variation of the popular Cosmopolitan. I suppose we'll be seeing Applepolitans, Strawberripolitans, Lemonpolitans, and maybe Chocopolitans soon enough.

Razz-Ma-Tazz

1½ oz. Vodka
½ oz. Chambord
1½ oz. Club Soda

Serve over ice in a tall glass, chilled.

Red-Headed Slut

½ oz. Jagermeister
½ oz. Peach Schnapps
½ oz. Cranberry Juice

Shake over ice and strain into a shot glass.

A relative of the Surfer on Acid.

Root Beer

1 part Kahlua
1 part Galliano
1 part Cola
1 part Beer

Combine in a shot glass.

Salt Lick

1¼ oz. Vodka
2 oz. Bitter Lemon Soda
2 oz. Grapefruit Juice

Pour ingredients over ice in a salt-rimmed wine glass.

Scotch 'n' Soda

1½ oz. Scotch
3 oz. Club Soda

Stir with ice.

Screwdriver

1¼ oz. Vodka
4 oz. Orange Juice

Add Vodka to a tall glass with ice and fill with Orange Juice.

Siberian Sunrise

1½ oz. Vodka
4 oz. Grapefruit Juice
½ oz. Triple Sec

Mix all ingredients with cracked ice in a shaker or blender.

Sicilian Kiss

1 oz. Southern Comfort
1 oz. Di Saronno Amaretto

Shake with ice and strain into a shot glass.

Silver Bullet

2 oz. Gin or Vodka
splash Scotch

Float Scotch on top.

Slippery Nipple

1 part Sambuca Romana
1 part Baileys

Shake with ice and strain into a shot glass.

Starry Night

¾ oz. Jagermeister
¾ oz. Goldschlager

Combine ingredients in a shot glass.

Jagermeister and Goldschlager should be stored in the fridge. If they are not ice cold, shake with ice and strain to make this shot.

Sweet Tart

1 oz. Absolut Vodka
¼ oz. Chambord
¼ oz. Rose's Lime Juice
¼ oz. Pineapple Juice

Shake with ice and strain into a shot glass.

Tequila Gimlet

1½ oz. Tequila
1½ oz. Rose's Lime Juice

Blend Tequila and Lime Juice with crushed ice and pour into a glass. Garnish with a Lime Wheel or Green Cherry.

Tequina

2 oz. Tequila
½ oz. Dry Vermouth

Stir Tequila and Vermouth with ice in a mixing glass until chilled. Strain into a chilled cocktail glass and garnish with a Lemon Twist.

Tom Collins

1½ oz. Gin
Juice of 1 Lemon
Club Soda

Shake first two ingredients and pour over ice. Top with Club Soda.

Topaz Martini

1¾ oz. Bacardi Limón
¼ oz. Martini & Rossi Extra Dry Vermouth
splash Blue Curaçao

Stir in a cocktail glass. Strain and serve straight up or on the rocks. Add a Lemon Twist or Olives.

John or Tom Collins?

John Collins, a waiter at Lipmmer's Old House on Coduit Street in Hanover Square, England, invented this drink. The name Tom was used instead of John because the drink was made with Old Tom Gin. Today, a John Collins is made with whiskey.

Trinity Martini

1 oz. Bombay Gin
½ oz. Sweet Vermouth
½ oz. Dry Vermouth

Stir in a cocktail glass. Strain and serve straight up or on the rocks. Add a Lemon Twist or Olives.

This cocktail is also known as the Trio Plaza Martini.

Tuaca Rocca

1 oz. Tuaca
1 oz. Peach Schnapps
1 oz. Vodka

Combine with ice in a rocks glass.

The Ultimate Tea

1½ oz. Irish Mist
Hot Tea

Pour Irish Mist in a warm glass. Fill with Hot Tea. Garnish with a Lemon Slice.

U-Z

¾ oz. Irish Mist
¾ oz. Baileys Irish Cream
¾ oz. Kahlua

Shake ingredients and strain into a shot glass.

Victoria's Secret

1½ oz. Magellan Gin
¾ oz. Apricot Brandy
1½ oz. Fresh Sour Mix
¼ oz. Campari

Shake ingredients with ice until cold. Strain into a chilled cocktail glass.

Created by Ray Srp, Bar Manager, Bellagio Hotel, Las Vegas, NV.

Vodka Martini

2 oz. Vodka
dash Dry Vermouth

Stir ingredients with ice and strain. Garnish with a Lemon Twist or an Olive.

You can also serve a Vodka Martini on ice.

Ward Eight

1¼ oz. Whiskey
4 dashes Grenadine
Juice of ½ Lemon

Shake ingredients with cracked ice and strain into a glass with finely cracked ice.

Watermelon

1 oz. Vodka
1 oz. Midori
2 oz. Orange Juice
2 oz. Cranberry Juice

Combine ingredients in a glass over ice.

White Russian

1½ oz. Vodka
½ oz. Kahlua
½ oz. Cream

Shake and serve over ice.

The origins of the Ward Eight

This drink is named after Boston's Ward Eight, known years ago for its bloody political elections. The drink is basically a Whiskey Sour with a splash of grenadine. Locke-O-Ber's in Boston is a great place to try one.

Wild Thanksgiving

1 part Wild Turkey
1 part Apple Brandy
splash Lime Juice
Cranberry Juice

Serve over ice with a Mint garnish.

Zipperhead

1 part Stolichnaya Vodka
1 part Chambord
1 part Club Soda

Combine in a shot glass with the Club Soda on top.

Zorbatini

1½ oz. Stolichnaya Vodka
¼ oz. Metaxa Ouzo

Stir gently with ice and strain. Garnish with a Green Olive.

Want more?

Visit **www.dummies.com/go/target** to get related articles, videos, or illustrated step-by-steps on your favorite Dummies title.

Making Everything Easier!
Guitar
ALL-IN-ONE
FOR
DUMMIES
8 BOOKS IN 1

Making Everything Easier!
Superfoods
FOR
DUMMIES
Learn to:
Brent Agin, MD
Shereen Jegtvig, MS

The Bible
FOR
DUMMIES
Michael Homan, PhD
A Reference for the Rest of Us!

Catholicism
FOR
DUMMIES
A Reference for the Rest of Us!

"A useful guidebook filled with clear instructions and helpful hints."
Meditation
FOR
DUMMIES
2nd Edition
Stephan Bodian
A Reference for the Rest of Us!

Happiness
FOR
DUMMIES
W. Doyle Gentry, PhD
A Reference for the Rest of Us!

Making Everything Easier!™
Personal Finance
FOR
DUMMIES
Learn to:
Eric Tyson, MBA

featuring coverage of the latest treatments
Diabetes
FOR
DUMMIES
3rd Edition
Alan L. Rubin, MD
A Reference for the Rest of Us!

Covers the iPhone, iPhone 3G, and iPhone 3G S!
3rd Edition
iPhone
FOR
DUMMIES
Learn to:
IN FULL COLOR!
Edward C. Baig
Bob "Dr. Mac" LeVitus

Making Everything Easier!™
iPod & iTunes
FOR
DUMMIES
Learn to:
Tony Bove